to: _____

from: _____

Published by Sellers Publishing, Inc.
Copyright © 2014 Sellers Publishing, Inc.
All rights reserved.

Front and back cover images © 2014 Ephemera
p. 4 © 2014 Postmark Press; p. 7 © 2014 Ephemera; p. 8 © 2014 Postmark Press; p. 11 © 2014
Ephemera; p. 12 © 2014 Ephemera; p. 15 © 2014 Ephemera; p. 16 © 2014 Ephemera; p. 19
© 2014 Ephemera; p. 20 © 2014 Postmark Press; p. 23 © 2014 Postmark Press; p. 24 © 2014
Ephemera; p. 27 © 2014 Postmark Press; p. 28 © 2014 Postmark Press; p. 31 © 2014 Postmark
Press; p. 32 © 2014 Postmark Press; p. 35 © 2014 Ephemera; p. 36 © 2014 Ephemera; p. 39
© 2014 Postmark Press; p. 40 © 2014 Ephemera; p. 43 © 2014 Postmark Press; p. 44 © 2014
Ephemera; p. 47 © 2014 Postmark Press; p. 48 © 2014 Postmark Press; p. 51 © 2014 Ephemera;
p. 52 © 2014 Postmark Press; p. 55 © 2014 Ephemera; p. 56 © 2014 Postmark Press; p. 59 ©
2014 Postmark Press; p. 60 © 2014 Postmark Press; p. 62 © 2014 Postmark Press.

Design by George Corsillo/Design Monsters

Sellers Publishing, Inc.
161 John Roberts Road, South Portland, Maine 04106
Visit our Web site: www.sellerspublishing.com
E-mail: rsp@rsvp.com

Credits appear on page 64.

ISBN 13: 978-1-4162-4516-2

No portion of this book may be reproduced or transmitted in
any form, or by any means, electronic or mechanical, including
photographing, recording, or by any information and storage
retrieval system, without written permission from the publisher.

10 9 8 7 6 5 4 3 2 1

Printed and bound in China.

The B Word

It Takes One to Know One!

Compiled by Robin Haywood

SELLERS
PUBLISHING

"Get in, bitch. We're going shopping."

"It's not that I hate you.
I just hope your next
period happens
in a shark tank."

"A word of advice:
Never play games with the
bitches who made the rules."

"If I was really a bitch, I'd make your life a living hell. Instead, I'll just watch you do that yourself."

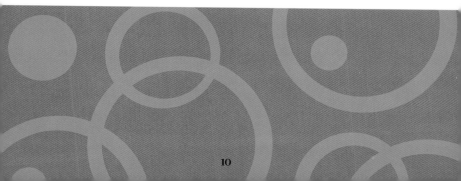

"I'll stop being a bitch
when men stop
being assholes."

"I do get called a
bitch quite often.
What I don't get called is
a pushover, a doormat,
stupid, sweetheart,
or dear. *Works for me.*"

"Whatever, I'm getting cheese fries."

"The sexiest parts
of my body? My brain,
my spine, and my guts."

"*Sorry.* We only carry sizes 1, 3, and 5. You could try Sears."

"We're not snobs, we're just better bitches than you!"

"I'm impressed. I've never met such a small mind inside such a big head."

"I can please only one person per day. Today is *not* your day. Tomorrow isn't looking good either."

"I wanted to make it a really special Valentine's Day, so I tied my boyfriend up. And for three solid hours I watched whatever I wanted on television."

"I feel like a brand-new bitch."

"I may be a cruel and heartless bitch, but at least I'm good at it."

"Women who pay their own rent don't have to be nice."

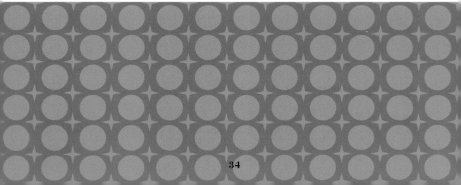

"My dear, I have kicked more ass than you have sat on."

"If you're going to
be a *serious* bitch,
be a classy one."

"I'm only as nice as people allow me to be, so don't push my bitch button and we'll be great."

"On Mondays, the bitches wear pink."

"If I had a dick, I'd be applauded and called a real man, but I'm a woman, so the world calls me a bitch."

"If you want high-performance women, we can go from zero to bitch in less than 2.1 seconds."

"Now we know why some bitches eat their children."

"I found my inner bitch
and ran with her."

"Some people call me a troublemaker. *Wrong.* I am a bitch who speaks the truth and won't put up with anyone's shit."

"When a man gives his opinion, he's a man. When a woman gives her opinion, she's a bitch."

"Save a boyfriend for a rainy day. And another, in case it doesn't rain."

"That's why her hair is so big. It's full of secrets."

"Yessir, we're 100% red-white-and-blue American bitches."

"I'd like to take the high road, but it would be so much more fun to take a detour and run your ass over."

Credits:

p. 5 unknown; p. 6 unknown; p. 9 unknown; p. 10 Sophie Monroe, from *Second Chance Romance*, 2013; p. 13 unknown; p. 14 unknown; p. 17 from *Mean Girls*, 2004. (Paramount Pictures, M. G. Films) Directed by Mark Waters, from the book *Queen Bees and Wannabes*, screenplay by Tina Fey; p. 18 unknown; p. 21 from *Mean Girls*, 2004. (Paramount Pictures, M. G. Films) Directed by Mark Waters, from the book *Queen Bees and Wannabes*, screenplay by Tina Fey; p. 22 unknown; p. 25 unknown; p. 26 Redders; p. 29 Tracy Smith, comedian; p. 30 unknown; p. 33 unknown; p. 34 Katherine Dunn; p. 37 unknown; p. 38 unknown; p. 41 unknown; p. 42 unknown; p. 45 unknown; p. 46 unknown; p. 49 unknown; p. 50 Courtney Love; p. 53 unknown; p. 54 Bette Davis; p. 57 Mae West; p. 58 from *Mean Girls*, 2004. (Paramount Pictures, M. G. Films) Directed by Mark Waters, from the book *Queen Bees and Wannabes*, screenplay by Tina Fey; p. 61 unknown; p. 63 unknown.